Snit Romney

An Satirical Take on the

Repugnicant
Candidate for President

BY JOHN F. INCE

Snit Romney: Repugnicant - Version 1.0

Updated: May 1, 2012

Published by: The Serendipity Publishing Group

Email: info@serendigity.com

© Serendigity Publishing Group, 2012

All Rights Reserved

ISBN-13: 978-1477446379

ISBN-10: 1477446370

Snit Romney on Twitter:

@SnitRomney or #Snit

Snit Romney's Facebook Page: www.SnitRomney.net

Snit Romney's Blog: www.SnitRomney.org

Snit Romney on Amazon: www.SnitRomney.com

To follow Repugnicants visit:

www.repugnicance.net

For bulk orders of this book email:

info@serendigity.com

Thanks to DonKeyHotey for the Cover Caricature of Mitt Romney: See
http://www.flickr.com/photos/donkeyhotey/5432732270/in/
set-72157625943276725/

The source image for this caricature is a Creative Commons licensed
image by Jessica Rinaldi from Mitt Romney Media via Wikimedia

---

Table of Contents

Introductory Stuff

MEET THE REAL SNIT - PAGE 23

Shakespeare on the Repugnicants

To-morrow, and to-morrow, and to-morrow,
Creeps in this petty pace from day to day,
To the last syllable of recorded time;
And all our yesterdays have lighted fools
The way to dusty death.
Out, out, brief candle!
Life's but a walking shadow, a poor player,
That struts and frets his hour upon the stage,
And then is heard no more. It is a tale
Told by an idiot, full of sound and fury,
Signifying nothing.

Macbeth, Act 5, Scene Five

What They're Saying About Snit Romney

• *Snit Romney* is the definitive parody of Mitt Romney. Based upon authoritative research, it surely will go down as one of the most influential pieces of political satire ever written.
 - *Mark Twain*

• This book has more bite than a $100 million ad buy. When the real Snit Romney really gets known, it will clinch my re-election.
– Barack Obooma

• *Snit Romney* is the best political parody to come out in years. We'll use it as the creative touchstone for our attack ads.
- Obama Campaign Manager, David Fluffe

• It's wicked good humor– chocked full of insight. I wish I'd spent my life doing something useful like writing satire instead wasting all that time running for President and inventing the Internet and re-inventing TV.
- Al Bore

• If Will Rogers were alive today this is the book he would write.
- USA Tomorrow

- *Snit Romney's* got the goods on Mitt Romney and the Repugnicants.
- Dan Blather

- *Snit Romney* captures shriveled spirit of Mitt Romney.
- Hairy Reed

- Personally, I didn't find this book very funny. It's just a lame prank and I know about lame pranks.
- Mutt Romney

- There are three things I didn't like about this book. It was too one sided. It was biased … and oops … I forgot the third thing?
- P. Rick Perry

- Destined to become a classic.
- Homer

A Mitt .. a Mutt ... or a Snit?

Choosing a name for a Mitt Romney caricature isn't an easy task. They're so many possibilities. To resolve the dilemma, I chose the politic thing to do ... I created a focus group - sort of. One Sunday, I took off on my bicycle and cruised around and about, coasting up to complete strangers, explained the nature of this epic project and then shoved a piece of paper in front of them with four names on it:

- ## Mutt Romney
- ## Snit Romney
- ## Mutt Romnoid
- ## Mitt Money

"Which one do you like best?" I asked.

This highly scientific poll included people of all ages, genders, blood types and shoe sizes – several hundred of them. The responses were about evenly split, with most saying that any  of the names would do just fine. Even some Republicans smiled. But there were a few ornery conservatives who were not amused. They openly expressed contempt – for me, my project, Democrats in general and Barack Obama in particular.

Fortunately for my safety, they were vastly outnumbered by those who felt that some form of Repugnicant Romneyesque caricature was desperately needed.

Why I'm not sure, but I think their passion for this project, has something to do with people loving the circus.

Dog owners uniformly preferred the name, "Mutt." They immediately thought of poor Seamus Romney and his ordeal while traveling over 1000 miles on the roof or the Romney Van. They have a point, on several levels. Mitt is a Mutt-like political mongrel, a cross breed of ideologies, who somehow barks at anybody who looks at him funny or challenges his flip-flopological philosophy.

Many respondents in my pedal poll were emphatic that Mitt **really** is a Snit. What exactly is a Snit? According to various Web sources, a Snit is, *a high strung person … a fit of anger ... a state of agitation or irritation ... an unreasonable fit of anger ... hissy fit. ... a person who is being really bitchy.*

At first, I hesitated in choosing *Snit* because I wasn't sure it hit the mark – until I dug deeper. While in the spotlight, Mitt projects methodical, highly disciplined, almost robotic persona. But when he not in the public spotlight, he's very high strung, and prone to get really peeved at people. As I studied transcripts and videos of his interviews, I could see distinct tendency towards hissy fits, especially when he encounters a question that confounds his thinking.

In the end, my choice of the name, Snit was sealed by watching one particular video. It was very revealing. During a break in a radio interview, when Mitt thought he was off mic and off camera, Mitt threw a Snit and the camera caught it all. It was a real hissy fit. The questioner was pushing Mitt's buttons on the matter of faith. The Mormon church, for those unfamiliar with its covenants, states clearly that anyone of the Mormon faith, who aids and abets those who get an abortion can be subject to disciplinary action from the church, presumably including excommunication.

As a lay Mormon leader, Mitt was originally against abortion, but soon found himself in a political pickle. When confronted by the liberal Massachusetts electorate in his campaign for Governor, he reversed course, which - natch - caused conservatives to question his authenticity. In this particular video, Mitt is asked about his shifting  abortion stances. At first he is calm and appears to be in control of the interview, until the interviewer starts reading from the Mormon Church laws. Slowly you see Mitt's face contorting. Suddenly he goes into major snit mode ... his arms waving wildly, attempting to gesticulate through arm movements what his mind couldn't quite articulate. In other words, Mitt Romney had no good response … and he morphed into Snit Romney.

This interview, and another on Fox News where Mitt throws another snit, give clues why Mitt has assiduously avoided the media throughout this entire campaign. Basically Mitt just  doesn't like being challenged on his record and he doesn't do very well hiding this fact? Unfortunately for the Snit, there are plenty of issues where his contradictory positions pose "challenges" shall we say … to his authenticity. Nuff said.

A Polarized Country Tacks to the Absurd

Belief it or not, the author of this ridiculous satire about Snit Romney was a Harvard Business School classmate of Mitt Romney. People who really know me are amazed that I graduated such an establishment school, because I made a conscious choice 25 years ago to step off the "Golden Path" well trodden by most graduates of HBS. I didn't know Mitt Romney back at Harvard Business School, but I'm pretty familiar with his alter ego, Snit Romney, having brought this caricature into the world of "literature" and nurtured the development of his persona with tender, loving care.

But let me be up front about why I wrote this satire, because it's ultimately rooted in serious purpose. The country is deeply polarized. Most of those on the extremes of the political spectrum have already made up their mind how they'll vote. But there is that swampland in the middle of the political spectrum, populated by independent thinkers who will likely determine the outcome of this election. So I wrote this book with three specific objectives in mind:

• to amuse and entertain those on the left,
• to piss off those on the right,
• to inform and nudge those in the middle.

It's just a gentle push I'm offering here, mostly for those who might have latent misgivings about Obama. I'm hoping that if they really think about this, they sure as Hell don't want Mitt Romney to be our next President. *In other words, I wrote this book as a "fair and balanced" appraisal of Mitt Romney – using the phrase to the full extent that it is used and abused on Fox News.*

The Sacred Tradition of Political Satire [1]

The tradition of political satire goes way back, all the way back to semi-sacred paintings in Paleolithic caves where images of horses were obviously intended to poke fun at tribal jackasses. Aristophanes' Greek plays were often satirical in nature. The leaders of Athens were fair game during the Peloponnesian War. Dante took potshots at political leaders in the "Divine Comedy,"

by placing them directly in Hell. Even Shakespeare is thought to have ridiculed Elizabethan politics in some of his plays, notably "Richard II." More recently, Mark Twain and Will Rogers stood out as eminent political satirists of their respective times. Now, prepare yourself for **Political Satire 2.0: The Rebranding of Mitt Romney as Snit Romney and the King of Bain.** Be sure to check out the other books in this highly Repugnicant political parody series:

• *Repugnicance: The 2012 Version of the Republican ~~Bible~~ Babble*
• *Repugnicants: The Wacky World of Republican Politics*
• *The Wiz of Iz: A Political Parable For Our Time.*

---

[1] Adapted from an article in Newsweek, Political Punch Lines, Sep 10, 2008, From ancient Greece to the modern day, people in power have been the subjects of our mockery.

One Overriding Theme: Repugnicance

These books are all unified by a one overriding satirical theme: Repugnicance. They're an attempt to beat the Republican candidates at their own branding game, by transforming them into ~~Republican~~ Repugnicant caricatures. I found this to be a remarkably easy and natural transition. With all their antics, the Republicans have created their own caricatures: Snoot Gingrich, Run Paul, P. Rick Perry, Herman Pizza, Rick Sanctimonious, Michele Babblethump and, of course, the Snit. Snit Romney, amazingly, is endowed with almost as much charisma as Mitt Romney, if you can imagine that. Surely it's the most parsimonious usage of charisma since Richard Nixon famously declared to a breathless nation, "I am not a crook!"

"FIRST MITT WON IOWA, THEN HE LOST IOWA?
THAT'S A CLASSIC ROMNEY FLIP-FLOP."
— STEPHEN COLBERT

Rebranding ~~Republicans~~ Repugnicants

Under the relentless assault of the Repugnicant attack machine, the Obama brand is now tarnished. Selling the same brand again this time around is a tough job. Obama's political strategists all but concede this. What then is their game plan for 2012? The strategy calls for a full frontal assault on the Republican / Mitt Romney brand, through coordinated series of attack ads relentless pushed in all media forms.

> IN 2008, MR. OBAMA ASSEMBLED A BROAD COALITION OF LIBERALS AND MODERATES TO PROPEL HIM TO AN EASY VICTORY. BUT HE FACES A MORE DIFFICULT TASK THIS TIME ENERGIZING THE LEFT, WHICH IS LOOKING FOR REASSURANCE THAT HE IS DEDICATED TO PROGRESSIVE ISSUES, WHILE ALSO APPEALING TO THE CENTER, WHICH WANTS TO SEE PARTISANSHIP IN WASHINGTON GIVE WAY TO RESULTS.
>
> - RICHARD W. STEVENSON, NY TIMES, 4/13/2012

In this series of wry and whimsical books, my objective is nothing less than to make Snit Romney and the Repugnicant brand household words. Every time someone hears the word Republican, I want their mind to immediately race towards the word Repugnicant. I want people to remember something very simple: Republicans and Mitt Romney are repugnant to democratic values, votes and virtues. But really, what is Repugnicance? Good question ....

What is Repugnicance?

• Repugnicance the official political religion of Snit Romney.

• Repugnicance is the Republican ~~Bible~~ babble demystified.

• Repugnicance is the translator between what comes out of the two sides of a Republican's mouth.

• Repugnicance is the gap between the rhetoric and reality of the Republican's talking points.

• Repugnicance is Republican blarney carried to its logically absurd extreme.

• Repugnicance is naked Republicanism, before their consultants dress it up with talking points manufactured by focus groups.

• Repugnicance is what you get when you strip away Republican campaign varnish and see through to their self serving policies.

• Repugnicance is what Republicans say to each other in private parties, after the beer has started flowing but before they open their mouths on the public airwaves.

• Repugnicance is the basis of a powerful new anti-Republican brand and the foundation of a Web 2.0 Movement for politics.

• Repugnicance the creative foundation of a citizen revolt against politics as usual.

• Repugnicance is the stuff of ridicule for the inmates of the asylum.

• Repugnicance is a political theatre of the absurd.

• Repugnicance an Occupy Movement for politics.

• Repugnicance is the imagination at work to re-engage those who have tuned out from politics.

My mission is to make it so that when anyone sees, hears or reads of Mitt Romney ... they immediately think of Snit Romney.

Political Reporters - An Ornery Breed

Having worked in the media off an on for over three decades, I know what reporters look for in a story. They want something that stands out from the stories written by other reporters in the pack. Political reporters are an especially ornery breed, because they've become cynical seeing how pols lie so naturally and how voter perceptions can be so easily manipulated. They want something that has an edge to it. They want something that's in the flow of what everybody is talking about, but forces people to see things from a different angle ... like Repugnicance

Imagine the Repugnicant movement, complete with bumperstickers, Youtube videos and photoshopped images. The themes, plot and characters are all there in public view to be played with by people with all kinds of creative talents.

Brands work when they touch a chord. They work when they're simple. They work when people instantly recognize them and what they're about. The satirical brands of Snit Romney and his merry band of Repugnicants might just touch that chord.

The brand of Repugnicance is designed to be virally extended in byte size pieces using all the tools of modern day social media. It will be largely Web based, but also stimulated by a gradual buildup to a Grand OLE Punditry (GOP) event – the Repugnicant National Unconvention. (RNU)

The Repugnicant National UnConvention

Mark Your Calendars
August 31 - Sept 2, 2012

Spliced between the Republican and Democratic Conventions, on the weekend of August 31-Sept 2, 2012, there will be another spectacle aptly dubbed the Repugnicant National UnConvention, (Twitter: #Repug) taking place on college campuses and select locations around the U.S.A. It will be extremely loosely coordinated by people who **really** don't know what they are doing – the esteemed body henceforth to be known as the Repugnicant National UnCommittee. This epochal event will serve as a truly ~~historical~~ hysterical fall campaign kickoff and an organizing vehicle for something so weirdly Repugnicant

… that … well … even I can't imagine what it might become.

Yes, it's a crazy idea … totally crazy and cool. Sometimes crazy is the only appropriate response to a political party that has gone weird on us … as Repugnicance has done. The Repugnicant National Unconvention will be an anti-Republican themed parody culminating in a theatre of the absurd. Students and other slightly touched participants, will play the roles of Republican caricatures like Snit Romney, Snoot Gingrich, P. Rick Perry, Run Paul, Saint Sarah and Donald Dump. These caricatures will go through the macabre motions of selecting a nominee for the Repugnicant Party.

Imagine this: loudly offensive music, skewered speeches, bastardized media interviews all converging in one huge event - Web coordinated ... an over-the-top political parody. Imagine an Occupy Movement for politics ... political theatre for the Internet age. Imagine live Webcasts of campus events, local Repugnicant conventions, all around the country. Facebook groups, Twitter Reddit links, news clips, YouTube videos all feeding into major media outlets. Anyone with a wit and a way can participate.

> # TRANSPARENT REPUBLICAN POLITICS IS KNOWN AS REPUGNICANCE.

The buildup to the RNU will take shape through the spring and summer of 2012 using social networks and YouTube videos, photoshopped images, T-shirts, bumperstickers - all the standard and non standard paraphernalia of political

campaigning.

On this localized, national stage, the RNU will be programmed for viral growth. The disenchanted and disenfranchised can voice their frustrations in a wry way that detracts major media attention. The goal here is to engage and empower those who are currently left out of the prevailing political equation.

Just like the GOP convention, the RNU will be strong on bombast and political vacuousness. Speakers will mouth political platitudes as Repugnicant gospel. Delegates will cast their votes for the most vapid candidate and we will have accomplished everything that was accomplished at the real Republican National Convention … nothing at all.

Although whimsical and a bit wacky, the RNU will also have a serious bite. It will expose Repugnicance as an absurd abstraction – an over the top political philosophy. It's the kind of thing Mitt Romney keeps talking about but nobody understands: *creative destruction* applied Mitt Romney in particular and to the Republicans in general. I can't wait?

Save the date, August 31-Sept 1, 2012 and set the stage for the political theatre in its most rapturous and riotous form. Rumor has it that George B. Wush and Dick Chicanery will come out from their caves to make guest appearances. John Stewart and Stephen Colbert won't be able to stay away.

SNIT ROMNEY BELIEVES THAT THE BEST WAY TO MOVE OUR COUNTRY FORWARD IS TO GO BACKWARDS.

Send in the Clowns

As the Republican Party tacts sharply towards the absurd, their candidates have swung towards the fences of self-caricature. It's a self-imposed exile from sanity, not only for Mitt Romney, but of the entire Republican circus. It's a party that's lost its way. It's a party that has veered so far to the right that its candidates often appear like clowns. They've all had their shining moments in the big top of politics: P.Rick Perry's "Opps" moment, Herman Pizza's abrupt revision of his 999 plan into his 696969 plan. Rick Sanctimonious sermons from the mount and Donald Dump's "Birther" bloopers. We should be grateful for the comic relief. Their exploits have potential not only for electrifying this election season, but also for transforming Republicanism into a VERY Repugnant parody of itself – a the new, improved brand of Repugnicance.

Democrats no longer have to beat Republicans at their own games. Repugnicants are beating themselves by re-branding themselves. How difficult can it be to imagine Mitt Romney as Snit Romney? It's a great entertainment value for the price of being American voter. The Repugnicant strategy of self parody is brilliant and we need only behold it in all its GOP grandeur. In other words, politics today is all about good entertainment. Let the show begin. Yee Haw!

After a year in which he was excoriated on an almost-daily basis by Mr. Romney and the others seeking the Republican nomination, Mr. Obama is now letting loose his competitive, street-ball side, mocking his opponent's vocabulary and suggesting a Republican victory would lead to social Darwinism. The comments by a Democratic strategist Wednesday night about Ann Romney's work history were condemned by Mr. Obama and his inner circle but only reinforced the sense that a lot Democrats are primed to play rough in 2012.

- Richard W. Stevenson, NY Times, 4/13/2012

Meet the

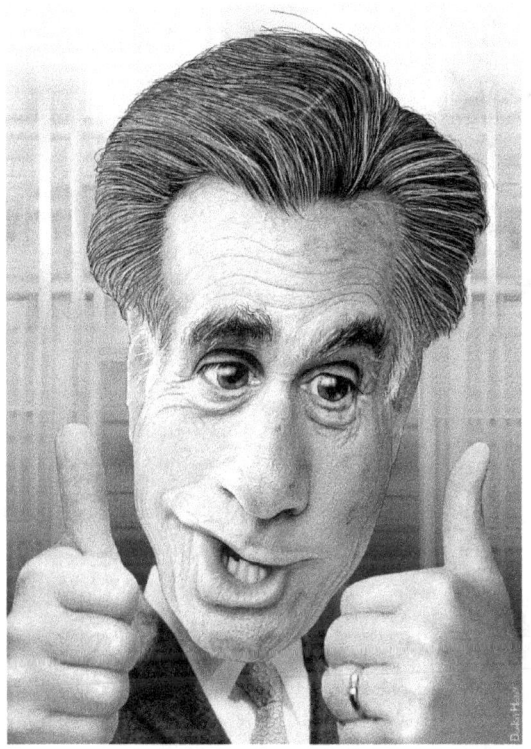

Real Snit

Mitt Romney and Snit Romney

Anybody who has followed Mitt's career as a politician has surely seen at least one of those priceless moments when Mitt  can't figure out who he is ... and then morphs into Snit. His identity crisis then emerges in full frontal view. It's the inevitable consequence of contradictory personalities slugging it out with each other. While one side of his brain is speaking to ultraconservatives, the other side is wooing moderates. He's made a noble attempt to pander to people off all stripes. To some extent all politicians today must do this dance. But with Obama at least you get the sense that there is a core set of beliefs that guide his actions. Sure Obama has to tact towards the center, perhaps a bit more than those on the far left would like, but the rapid veering of Mitt or Snit this way or that, depending on the audience and mood of the moment, is dizzying to anybody really paying attention ... all six of us not counting Mitt's army of paid consultants. The Snit is a cross breed of private equity, fundamentalist religion, social conservatism, and Olympic scale marketing.

It makes for surreal political drama. Can we take Mitt seriously, with any position he puts forth? Okay, times up ... Let's call a spade a spade: a Mitt is a Snit is a Mitt. So here we go ... into the realm of caricature following the improbable political story of the man who increasingly shall be known as Snit Romney. Welcome to the realm of political absurdity, soon to be seen as a very Repugnicant brand of politics.

***

Snit Romney - A Political Enigma

The candidate without a character ... the politician without a personality ... formerly the bane of Venture Capital ... bought early into in Staples: The Office Superstore, but now wants to redecorate the Oval office as corporate annex ... says he understands how the economy works ... but has only seen how it works from the top down ... specialized in buying companies and firing their employees ... now claims he's an expert in creating jobs ... what? ...

Mormon missionary work in France helped shape his character ... now trying to fit the rounded shape of Mormonism into the square holes of Christinsanity ... saved the Olympics from disgrace by selling it to socially challenged sponsors like Nike ... flip flopper supreme ... switches positions with alarming frequency ... now disavows any connection to the ObamaCare health care system he instituted en Mass ... attended exclusive Cranberry School in Bloomfield Hills where every student is plum ... father was Governor of Michigan ... he would have done the same but took the wrong, right turn out of Haavid Yard ... owns so many blind trusts he can no longer see straight ... can't live down the Seamus Romney canine caper ... a sad story of a freaked out Irish setter traveling on a box on top of the van ... the story catapults Snit to the top echelons of American political satire. But, we're just getting started? Stay tuned. There's more.

Snit Romney, The Prissy Pissy Candidate

In his book, *No Apology*, Mitt Romney takes the media to task for not holding the candidates accountable for their evasive statements and positions. He writes, "In one of our Republican primary debates, for example, we were asked, 'What would you do to fix Social Security?' Most responded by restating the problem–Social Security is bankrupt–rather than by addressing a solution; politicians have learned from experience that it is 'unwise to address the third rail of American politics.' But why is that? Why is it that the media doesn't hold those accountable who duck this critical issue?"

When I read that I thought to myself, *this guy is really good*. During the long primary battle he assiduously avoided the media - giving only a couple of interviews and then only to friendly, hand picked reporters at Fox and elsewhere. Then he head fakes. After refusing to meet with the media, he chews them out because they don't hold the candidates accountable. Wow! He's got this campaign thing down pat.

In the following fictional exchange between Mitt Romney and *The Washington Pissed,* I live out my fantasy interview with Mitt Romney. It's the interview where his alter ego, Snit Romney, the high strung, prissy, pissy candidate, who doesn't hide who he really is, started to take shape in my mind.

Mitt Romney Loses It

Morphs Into Snit Romney

SPECIAL TO THE WASHINGTON PISSED

Washington Pissed: Does granting this interview finally mean that you're warming up to the media?

Mitt Romney: Not really! Once you've achieved status in society like I have, you no longer have an obligation to mingle with the little people. ... people of small minds ... like you and the rest of the mindless media. I'm here because my handlers told me to be here. I pay them big bucks so I've got to listen to them.

Washington Pissed: Good point. But if you're a candidate for President, you've got to do it ... that's if you want the voters to have some idea of who you really are, beneath your plastic exterior.

Mitt Romney: Excuse me? Beneath my plastic exterior?

Washington Pissed: Yeah! Some say that you're afraid that the Romney brand might be damaged by answering real questions about what you really believe and feel. Conservative voters in the

primaries might see you're really not a conservative. More liberal voters in the general election might see you're really not a liberal. The net result is that everybody now thinks you don't really have any core convictions and the Romney brand has been irreparably damaged. Any comment?

Mitt Romney: I don't want to dignify your thoughts with a comment. I don't even know what you mean by the Romney Brand.

Washington Pissed: Yes you do. It's the brand your consultants have created. You're being sold to the voters warmed over fillet steak. Unfortunately the Romney brand doesn't taste so good to the voter's palates. Your difficulty selling yourself in the primaries just might be sending you a  message. The voters want anybody but Romney. The Mitt brand isn't selling well on the menu of politics.

Mitt Romney: We'll see whether it washes out in the general election. We like the new Etch-a-Sketch, Romney brand that we're about to roll out to the voters. It's a tasty brand ... it's a clean brand ... a consistent brand ... and an aggressive brand ...

Washington Pissed: Yes, but it's also the brand that has many people asking, "Who is this guy?"

Mitt Romney: I am who I am and my character is now out there in full view, thanks to muckracking media outlets like yours.

Washington Pissed: Okay, we since your brought it up, let's talk for a moment about this "prank" you played on one of the gay students at the exclusive Cranbrook School where you prepped. According to multiple eyewitnesses, you lead a gang of fellow students, pinned him to the floor and snipped his newly dyed blonde hair with scissors. The guy was terrified and the incident scarred his life. He later just disappeared from the school. And nothing happened to you. What were you thinking?

Mitt Romney: Oh that was just a little hi-jinx … just a jolly little prank … we were having fun … you know boys will be boys.

Washington Pissed: Hi-jinx? Prank? Fun? Mitt, in another set of circumstances, you would have been arrested for assault and thrown in jail. What does this say about your inner bully?

Mitt Romney: Oh come on … don't get carried about with your psycho-babble on this thing. It was forty eight ago. I'm a new person now.

Washington Pissed: Perhaps, but your inner bully came out in other forms at Bain Capital. You just learned how to monetize your aggressive behavior. Your insensitivity became an asset when you took over companies and then fired workers, all in the interest of profits. Any comment?

Mitt Romney: That's just creative destruction, which, if you know anything at all about business, is completely justified by sound business practices. Just ask my old profs at Harvard Business School.

Washington Pissed: So you're basically saying that what you did at Cranbrook School to that kid and to businesses at Bain Capital was okay.

Mitt Romney: Okie do-key … okay …. just part of the game. Ha Ha. Ha. Don't you have a sense of humor?

Washington Pissed: I can see we're getting nowhere with this. Let's shift tact to your tendency to do a delicate dance around uncomfortable incidents and difficult policy issues. The record

---

shows your positions have changed with a l a r m i n g frequency.

Mitt Romney: My record?

W a s h i n g t o n Pissed: Yes. Your public record.

Snit Romney: My public record is not as public as you think it is. We have staff scrubbing and sanitizing almost everything I've said and done in public for the last 20 years.

Washington Pissed: Yes, I understand you had your staff remove all the hard drives from their computers before you left office in Massachusetts in 2008. And that raised eyebrows. You've also refused to release your earlier tax returns and the names of the "bundlers" who raise big bucks for your campaign. This makes you seem controlling or, shall we say, less than transparent. What are you trying to hide?

Mitt Romney: My financial information is my own business.

Washington Pissed: So you're basically saying that you want to keep both your finances and your character flaws hidden from public view.

Mitt Romney: Listen … I don't need to respond to your questions. I'm doing this interview because my handlers told me too … not because … I don't need sh.….

Washington Pissed: (Interrupting) Do you ever get mad, I mean like really pissed? Do you have any personality beneath that veneer?

Mitt Romney: Personality?

Washington Pissed: Yes, is there a "there" there?

Mitt Romney: What there are you referring to there?

Washington Pissed: Okay, so …, there really is no there, there. Let me shift tact again. Why should anyone vote for you?

Mitt Romney: Because my public persona is so well constructed by my media team. My brand is acceptable in spite of my lack of charisma or an effervescent personality … more acceptable than that other guy … for sure.

Washington Pissed: So you admit to having character flaws?

Mitt Romney: I might as well … every time I open my mouth you blowhards say I've just flip flopped.

Washington Pissed: But isn't that what you do?

Mitt Romney: No Comment.

Washington Pissed: I see … you don't want to play. So let's take Obama Care. What do you think of that? Were you for it or against it?

Mitt Romney: No Comment.

Washington Pissed: Hello? Earth to a Romnoid … any human trace inside there? Is there anyone inside ... anyone who feels passion about anything? Is there a human being inside who gets angry? Why are you so afraid to show your emotions? Showing emotion just might convince the voters that you're not a fake. You're getting red in the face now. Are you getting angry?

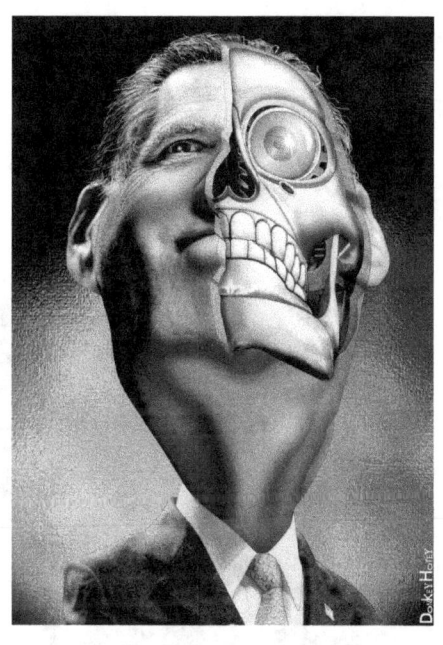

[**Mitt Romney's face contorts and slowly a new persona emerges.**]

Snit Romney: I'm not angry… I'm just having a Snit.

Washington Pissed: Well Snit away. Maybe soon we'll find a real person concealed in there. You're actually starting to show some real emotion now. Just out of curiosity, what do Mormon's do when they get mad, since they're not supposed to swear.

Snit Romney: Mormon's discourage swearing, but it's not a covenant. Personally I look at swearing as a loss of self control… not a Mormon dictate. Besides, my Mormon faith is a private matter. It shouldn't be a relevant consideration for the voters.

Washington Pissed: But it is. In fact, there were even some fundamentalist Christians who were willing to vote for an adulterer like Snoot Gingrich rather than a Mormon. What do you say to that?

S n i t R o m n e y: F...k them!

Washington Pissed: I beg your pardon?

S n i t R o m n e y: You heard what I said. F...k them!

Washington Pissed: Oh … I see where you're headed with this. You're showing everybody your Mormon faith doesn't bind you.

But this looks like another flip flop … this one coming at the expense of your Mormon faith. Right?

Snit Romney: F..k you.

Washington Pissed: Your dark side is coming through now. Is this why your handlers keep you on such a tight leash?

> **Snit Romney:** F...k yeah!
>
> **Washington Pissed:** There we go … finally we're scratching the beneath the surface … maybe there really is a human being behind the door? Keep it up … the voters are warming up to you now!
>
> **Snit Romney:** F...k you!

Washington Pissed: We're making real progress now! Can we assume that the real person beneath your highly polished campaign persona feels true passion when he says, "F...k you?"

Snit Romney: F...k yeah!

Washington Pissed: You don't wish to say anything else but F… them ... F…k you, and F..k yeah?

Snit Romney: F...k no!

Washington Pissed: Thank you Governor! It's been a real pleasure getting to know you better. Is this why you don't like to talk to the media?

Snit Romney: F...k this! I'm outta here!

"Hookers in Times Square, God bless 'em, are offering a Mitt Romney Special. For an extra $20 they'll change positions."
— David Letterman

The CEO of U. S. Inc.

Mitt Romney's father, Hugh Romney, was CEO of American Motors. Snit Romney was CEO of Bain Capital and now he wants to be CEO of American Inc. ... Snit Romney touts himself as a businessman who knows what it takes to get the engine of America humming again. The Romney vision sees the ascendance of a corporatized country in which power flows top down. His vision is blurry, though, when he set his eyes upon the forces of political and economic democracy.

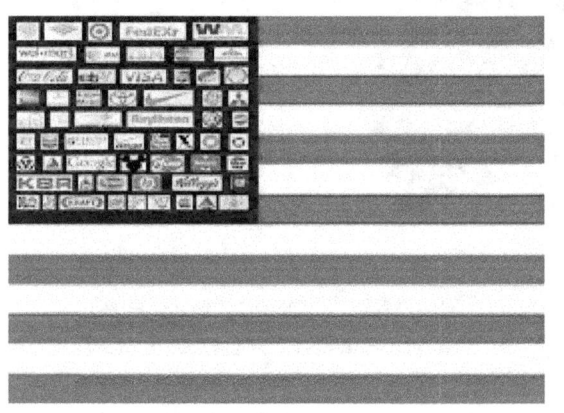

His goal is to remake America in the image of Bain Capital - a world is which the "creative destruction" touted by professors at Harvard Business School, leaves entire swaths of the economy writhing in economic pain, as income flows from the bottom up to the Mitt Romney's of the world.

> ## ANYBODY WHO'S REALLY WATCHING CAN'T HELP BUT SEE MITT ROMNEY'S POLITICAL IDENTITY CRISIS EMERGING IN THE PERSONA OF SNIT ROMNEY.

Poll: 63% Of Americans Say They Have A Problem With A Mormon President Who Is Also Mitt Romney

WASHINGTON—A Gallup poll released Tuesday suggests voters are highly resistant to electing a Mormon who is Mitt Romney as president of the United States. "I'm already hesitant to vote for a Mormon, and I'm especially uncomfortable if that Mormon is Mitt Romney," said Wyoming voter Dale Butler, 63, adding that he needed only the slightest extra excuse not to vote for a Mormon candidate, and that the candidate in question being Mitt Romney "probably sealed the deal." "I don't expect anyone to be perfect, but in the end, I just don't think I can overlook the fact that someone is both a Mormon and Mitt Romney. Personally, that's just too much for me." The same poll revealed that voters were more than willing to overlook the serial philandering of a candidate who was not also Newt Gingrich. 2

---

2 Courtesy of the Onion - http://www.theonion.com/articles/poll-63-of-americans-say-they-have-a-problem-with,27539/

Mitt Romney Debates Snit Romney

BUTTING HEADS AND PRECARIOUSLY MAKING THEIR WAY THROUGH THE REPUBLICAN BABBLE, HERE'S A VERY REPUGNICANT DEBATE BETWEEN MITT 'N SNIT.

Mitt Romney: To be perfectly blunt, your multiple personalities have a communication problem with each other. Snit, why don't the two sides of your mouth talk to each other more?

Snit Romney: Listen Mitt, I don't have multiple personalities. I am who I am, a man of constancy. And I'm candidate is the best qualified to be President, because I've been in business my whole life, except for the parts of my life when I was wasn't.

Mitt Romney: Okay I grant you that point. Maybe you don't have multiple personalities. Maybe you don't even have one personality. Maybe you're just a political robot pretending to be a candidate.

Snit Romney: You should talk. You've been programmed by your handlers to say anything that might appeal to whoever you're talking to at the moment.

Mitt Romney: Me? What about you? Mr. Hissy Fit – You're the most peevish candidate in the race. You take offense at the smallest slight.

Snit Romney: My skin is plenty thick enough to stand up to your to political attacks. I can take it and shovel it out. You know Mitt, you're really a Mutt. You're nothing but a political mongrel.

Mitt Romney: No, you're describing yourself? Your positions are all over the political map. In Iowa and other conservative states, you cast yourself as a conservative of convenience. But in your home state of Massachusetts, you look more like a Dukakis liberal. Do you have any core convictions?

Snit Romney: I have many core convictions ... so many I can't keep them all straight. You're the flip flopper. Na Na Na Na Na Na.

Mitt Romney: You just proved my point. As soon as I started attacking you, you had a snit.

Snit Romney: You attacked me first, instead of addressing the real issues in this campaign.

Mitt Romney: Oh, is this campaign about real issues? I thought it was about character. That's why. I'm a man of stability, discipline and consistency.

Snit Romney: Sure you are, Mitt. Totally consistent about your opposition to Obama Care, but ... wait ... in your book you wrote that you supported the Health Care legislation in Massachusetts that, you wrote, should become a national model.

Mitt Romney: It's you who's confused. Are you for the individual mandate or against it. If you're against it, why is it the law in Massachusetts?

Snit Romney: I'm 100% opposed to Obama Care. It's a disaster. ... and I've been consistent about that position as far back as the last time I changed my thinking about it.

Mitt Romney: So do you agree or disagree with me! **Is** Obama Care is going to add trillions to the national debt at a time when we can least afford it, or is it what the country needs to reduce costs.

Snit Romney: Let me clarify my shifting positions. I knew it would be a disaster and that's why we passed it in Massachusetts?

Mitt Romney: Oh, I understand now. Let me recap. Obama Care has some good things in it. The parts of it that are consistent with what we did in Massachusetts are based on sound thinking. We need to find a way to provide health coverage to the millions of American's who today are not covered, but they shouldn't have to pay for it. When they get sick, we all have to pay for their care. That's just not fair to the rest of us.

Snit Romney: So there you go again ... isn't that what you wrote in your book, until you changed it?

Mitt Romney: I've never wavered on this point. I know what I wrote in my book. I know that I didn't come out for the individual mandate, in my book or in any public statements since the.

Snit Romney: I read your book too. In fact, I'm in it. I was in there when it came out in the hardcover edition of the book, but you took me out of the paperback.

> "Many voters feel that Mitt Romney is out of touch with real Americans after he tried to make a bet with Rick Perry for $10,000. When asked to comment, Mitt said, 'I'm sorry, but that's all I had in my pocket at the time.'" – Conan O'Brien

Mitt Romney: $10, 000 says you're wrong.

Snit Romney: I'll take that bet and bump you $20,000.

Mitt Romney: Okay, I'll raise you another $20,000. Hey, I'm successful. I've got a ton of dough. I know how the economy works. I'm successful and no apologies about that. I win all my bets and I'll win this one.

What, is that a lot of money to you people?

Snit Romney: You're on … and we'll let the voters decide about this one.

Mitt Picks Snit as Running Mate

Salt Lake City, Utah - In a surprise move going against over two-hundred years of tradition, Republican-candidate Mitt Romney announced today that Snit Romney would be his Vice-Presidential running mate. While the two candidates appear to be the same person, Mitt Romney is known to have two opinions of any issue at any given time. "Some might argue this is the most arrogant Vice-Presidential pick since Dick Cheney's search found only himself. I also did a lot of soul searching and realized my core beliefs were definitely two different people depending on the polling of the day, sometime five," Mitt Romney stated at a recent campaign stop in Texas. "Why, if I really think about, and all the positions I have taken, I could probably fill out the my Cabinet as well."

According to Constitutional historian Lloyd Beenwasser, there is no rule against a candidate choosing his alter ego. "Well, to be honest, the Founding Fathers were men of political conviction, who at the end of the day developed our democratic framework after years of debate and philosophical thought. Romney just goes by what the polls say, a ship set sail on the zeitgeist of ever-changing public opinion," Beenwasser said, while thumbing through law book after law book to see how this could possibly be legal. ...

Romney is expected to formal announce Romney as the pick later today at a news conference at his family's sprawling estate, which should have more than enough room for all the Mitt Romneys planning to attend. As of press time, there is no word if they would all be wearing the same magic underwear. [3]

[3] Adapted from a post by Daily Kos member, Patience John - http://www.dailykos.com/story/2012/04/12/1082815/-Romney-Picks-Romney-as-VP

Tips on Traveling With Your Dog

Although Mitt Romney now famous "Roof Roof Seamus" incident happened over 25 years ago, it's a story that still dogs his campaign. Poor Seamus, the Irish setter who puked when Mitt Romney strapped him on the roof of his car for 12 hours. It's now become a tale of ~~historical~~ hysterical proportions. This simple story has spawned an entire movement: *Dogs Against Romney.* That's a lot of barking. Late-night host David Letterman has jumped on the dogwagon with nightly jabs. Parody Web videos have proliferated. You can buy your own, "Dogs Aren't Luggage" T-shirts or join nearly 50,00 others on the "Dogs Against Romney Facebook Page."

How will this shaggy dog story end? Nobody knows. Seamus' legacy lives on in the hearts and minds of dog lovers everywhere. If the Snit loses by whisker, in 2012, he will have only himself to thank for the puke that he induced on his traveling Repugnicant road show.

> "PETA IS NOT HAPPY THAT MY DOG LIKES FRESH AIR." - MITT ROMNEY, ON STRAPPING HIS DOG TO THE TOP OF THE CAR."

Amazing Things Said By Snit Romney

• "Back in high school I did some dumb things and if anybody was hurt by that or offended by that I apologize. If I did stupid things, I'm afraid I've got to say sorry for it." (Romney's quasi-apology on FOX News for the incident when he lead classmates at the Cranbrook School in an assault on a gay student.)

• "I saw my father march with Martin Luther King." (Romney's campaign later admitted that they didn't march on the same day, or in the same city)

• "My sons are all adults and they've made decisions about their careers and they've chosen not to serve in the military and active duty and I respect their decision in that regard. One of the ways my sons are showing

support for our nation is helping me get elected because they think I'd be a great president."

• "I purchased a gun when I was a young man. I've been a hunter pretty much all my life." (Romney's campaign later said he'd been hunting twice, once when he was 15, and once in 2006 at a Republican fundraiser

• "I'm not a big-game hunter. I've made that very clear. I've always been a rodent and rabbit hunter. Small varmints, if you will."

• "Hugo Chavez has tried to steal an inspiring phrase 'Patria o muerte, venceremos.' It does not belong to him. It belongs to a free Cuba." -invoking a phrase that translates to "Fatherland or death, we shall overcome," which Fidel Castro has used to close his speeches for years, and which is associated with Cuban oppression.

• "Well, the question is kind of a non sequitur, if you will. And what I mean by that -- or a null set." --after being asked during a Republican debate whether is was a mistake to invade Iraq

• "We should double Guantanamo!"

• "I'm happy to learn that after I speak you're going to hear from Ann Coulter. That's a good thing. I think it's important to get the views of moderates."

REPUGNICANCE IS A BASTARDIZED SATIRE OF THE REPUBLICAN

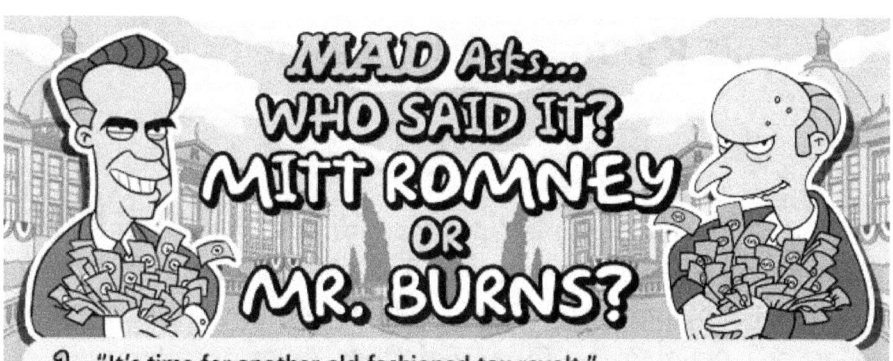

MAD Asks...
WHO SAID IT?
MITT ROMNEY
OR
MR. BURNS?

1. "It's time for another old-fashioned tax revolt."

2. "I've always been a rodent and rabbit hunter. Small varmints, if you will."

3. "So, what shall we do tomorrow? Go grousing?"

4. "I'm not concerned about the very poor."

5. "Why do I need another penny? I have billions."

6. "Corporations are people, my friend!"

7. "I like being able to fire people who provide services to me."

8. "I'm really enjoying this so-called 'iced cream.'"

9. "I tasted a beer and tried a cigarette once, as a wayward teenager, and never did it again."

10. "I grew up drinking Vernors and watching ballgames at Michigan & Trumbull."

11. "A blue-collar bar! Let's go slumming!"

12. "I have some great friends that are NASCAR team owners."

13. "I'm running for office, for Pete's sake — I can't have illegals!"

14. "This anonymous clan of slack-jawed troglodytes has cost me the election."

Romney: 1, 2, 4, 6, 7, 9, 10, 12, 13   Burns: 3, 5, 8, 11, 14   **MAD**

Theidiotical.com

Snit Romney's Direct Line to God

Dear God:

As the only really Repugnicant candidate for President of the Untied States of America, I truly represent the hopes and dreams of private equity executives everywhere. In this capacity I am also the Chief Interpreter of the Repugnicant ~~Bible~~ Babble. Repugnicance sits upon the cross of high finance and fundamentalist Christianity. In this sense, Repugnicance is a miracle. How else can anybody explain how these two minds sets could mesh in any one mind?

Repugnicance is just now coming into its own as a modern day religion. It hasn't alway been as powerful a force as it is now. The unfortunate result was the election of Barack Obama, which we all now know was a disaster of epochal proportions for rich people, despite the appreciation of stocks in my portfolio during this his Presidency.

SO, NOW WHAT DO WE DO...?

Of the major political religions, Repugnicance is the only one that emphatically endorses the Almighty buck as our savior. All this has been so beautifully expressed in the Repugnicant ~~Bible~~ Babble.

As you may be aware, some Christian Conservatives, don't feel that my particular brand of Christianity is as legitimate as theirs. I am writing you now to ask for your endorsement so that I can finally close the deal. I could also use your help with the inspiration thing. Somehow, I just don't seem to be connecting with them. I need your help to get them to come out in flocks to the voting booths in November 2012.

My Repugnicant positions are like finely chiseled stone sculptures of your only begotten son, Jesus Christ, who died for our political sins on the cross of Democrapic rhetoric. To wit, all true Repugnicants:
• fight for the right for our children to pray in school.
• recognize that cutting taxes is the Godly thing to do.
• heed your advice to reduce the size of government.
• cringe when we see gays serving openly in the military.
• feel queasy every time a same sex marriage is performed.
• And did we mention cutting taxes?

We know that you do not always approve of everything that we humans do because we are born sinners in the Garden of Eden. But the Democraps really take things too far. For that reason we ask that you look askance at Obama's political machine this election cycle and smite Democraps down in their tracks. We need all the Super PAC money we can raise to diminish the amount of traction they gain both politically and spiritually. This is clearly be a wise investment of your time, energy and spiritual capital. Remember, Repugnicants we are specifically focused on the things that matter most to you.

We wholeheartedly endorse your positions on faith. We know that life is sometimes difficult, that that's just your way of giving us a quiz. Right? And Repugnicants have passed the quiz because we have suffered the slings and arrows of

misfortune during the trying times of the Obama years.

Now the future is s h a p i n g   u p differently. Isn't it amazing how far we have progressed since four years ago when Obama was seen as a "charismatic savior."

To counter his atheistic poppycock, we my campaign is pushing ahead with religious zeal to promote tax cuts and a revival of the Supply Side Economics sub-religion. We have ideas in foreign policy, health care, anti-socialism. Your support for us will be instrumental in our victory at the ballot box in November 2012. What do you say? Will you join our team?

Sincerely yours,

Snit P. Romney
The Repugnicant Candidate for President of the Untied States of America

GOD'S AUTHENTIC REPLY!

Dear Mr. Romney:

At this critical juncture in evolution of humanity, I am concerned about things. I can clearly see that we need something dramatic to shift the course of history. I am prepared to take extreme karmic action to that effect. That's why I look kindly upon your creation of a new and improved Repugnicance brand political philosophy. I knew that if humanity was to survive, a new kind of wisdom and a much more potent quasi religious - political movement must be thrust on the world stage.

Accordingly I have decided, for the first time in the history of the world, to endorse a political brand in the upcoming election for President. I believe it is incumbent on me as God let the masses know where I stand by endorsing Snit Romney and his brand of Repugnicance. as the **Salvation of humanity**. You may use this letter as evidence to this effect. Good luck as you seek to interpret the 2012 version of The Repugnicant Holy ~~Bible~~ Babble.

Sincerely yours,

God

The Ten Commandments of Repugnicance

THE ALMIGHTY DOLLAR IS THE LORD YOUR GOD
AND HATH BROUGHT YOU OUT OF
THE HOUSE OF BONDAGE.

$ ONE: Thou shalt have no other gods besides the Almighty dollar.

$ TWO: Thou shalt make for thyself a campaign image -- the likeness of which is everything on television, or that's on the Internet, or that's in the media in any form.

$ THREE: Thou shalt not take the name of Snit Romney in vain.

$ FOUR: Thou shalt remember the election day, and keep it holy.

$ FIVE: Thou shalt honor thy lobbyists and thy campaign contributors.

$ SIX: Thou shalt murder any legislation proposed by Democraps.

$ SEVEN: Thou shalt commit ideological adultery.

$ EIGHT: Thou shalt steal from government coffers.

$ NINE: Thou shalt bear false witness against Democraps.

$ TEN: Thou shalt covet thy lobbyists campaign contributions; Thou shall covet thy lobbyists wallet, his portfolio, his car, his corporate jet, his vacations, and anything that's thy lobbyists.

Snit Romney's
Virtual Town Meeting

The Repugnicant Babble Explained in Plain Gibberish

What Is Your Position on Foreign Policy?

• Question From: Andrew Babcock, Mechanic, Sioux City, Iowa

SNIT'S RESPONSE: Let me back up and approach this question from a rational perspective. Increasingly "liberal experts" believe that we rapidly approaching "peak chaos in the world." Some of them even believe we have already reached it ignoring the bungling leadership of Barack Obama. We don't know where we are in this regression. The scientific data is unclear. Peak chaos signals the moment at which the maximum supply of chaos is reached and global confusion starts to increase exponentially. Common sense starts reverse proportionality. Peak chaos also signals that God emphatically states to humankind,

"Hold it folks, You're not doing things right." Will these factors a f f e c t A m e r i c a ' s strength as a world leader and our ability to sustain e c o n o m i c growth on a p a r the appreciation of my stock portfolio? It's a question that we need to ask. Otherwise economic reckoning of epic proportions awaits us. Will historians one day look back at this moment in time and say, "You blew it folks!" I see a different future for America. I believe there is a better way to organize world affairs based upon the creative use of debt, leverage and other miraculous innovations in high finance. Further details of my foreign policy agenda are available in my book, *No Apology, No Plan, No Nothing.*

What Are The Planks of Your Platform?

• Question By: Martha Kempis, Grocery Store Clerk, Flat Creek, Kentucky

Snit's Response: My Platform is based upon what I call the 5 Gs!

God: I support God wholeheartedly in his various religious forms and will advance religious policy initiatives despite what Democrapic atheists and non believers disbelieve about my faith.

Guns: I support the rights of gunslingers and red blooded Americans to carry and shoot as many guns as they want at whatever they want so including shooting holes through The Constitution.

Gays: I believe that a man and a woman are just that ... and not to be confused with other kinky behaviors in bed or whatever.

Gold: The specter of fiscal irresponsibility with the looming crisis of the dollar is coming ... but not if you place your trust deposits in my campaign coffers. Hey, we'll all get rich during my terms in office.

Government: Enough is enough and too much is too much. When government becomes part of the problem that it's trying to solve, then you have a rubrics' cube of creative destruction that, in the end, serves no one but the pork barrels and their lobbying cronies inside the beltway of our great nation's capitol.

Why is Modern Politics So Repugnicant?

• Question From: Gertrude Wister, Air Traffic Controller, San Jose, CA

SNIT'S RESPONSE: Good question! Political paralysis is a fact of modern life. But there's now a new political wind blowing called Repugnicance. Soon everybody will want a piece of the equity. Until then, we've a problem. I admit, different people have different ideas about what Repugnicance means inaction. There are those who feel action means inaction. Some think it's the reverse. I believe that the President has to sort it all out and dole out favors accordingly. I intend to take the "bull of change" by the horns and wrestle it to the ground. Down here inside Repugnicance Power Bunker, we believe that you "can't change change itself," without getting splinters.   T   h   e fractured groups within the grander Repugnicance movement (namely: The Tea Party) don't believe anything that can't be proved. Some flip

GOP field comes into focus

floppers believe that they can have it both ways and still get theirs. I'm not one of them. Well, maybe I am.

On the other hand, I believe that all this talk about me flip flopping is nonsense! My consistent inconsistency has been a constant. It's what strong leadership is all about. We need to take Democraps out behind the woodshed, and give them a stern talking to about their increasingly socialist tendencies, not to mention questions about their place of birth. Did I just say that? No, I didn't and you can read the record. Coming back to the sorry and sordid of politics today, I intend to run a positive campaign, except for the parts that are negative. All this will become clear as this campaign unfolds and the facts speak for themselves. I call upon the mainstream media, to get it right and stop reporting as if this were just a horse race. The great country of our deserves better and I intend to give it to them.

What is your position on Health Care?

• Question From: Eleanor Throttlemeyer, Second Grade Teacher, Bloomington, IN

SNIT'S RESPONSE: My position on health care has been very clear since day one. My other position on health care is even more clear. This debate centers on one overriding issue: do we want good health care or not? The Democrats answer was 3000 pages of convoluted gibberish to pass a sweeping government takeover of health care.

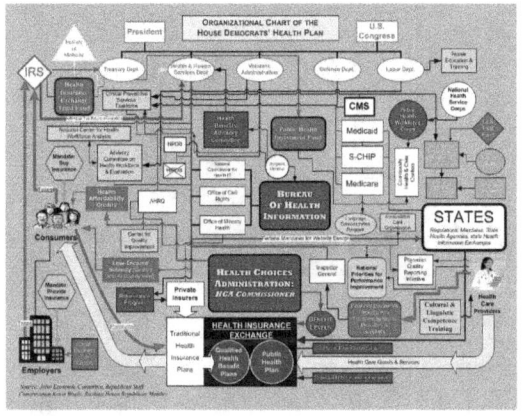

That's what we're up against in this debate. The president and Democraps in Congress need to start over on their health care plan, with a plan is more like the one I promoted, which coincidentally is nearly identical to the one they passed. Reasonable Repugnicants are ready to work on bipartisan solutions to health care reform, as long as the solutions are all ours.

In an effort to clear up his reputation as a flip-flopper, Mitt Romney will give a speech on health care. And then, right afterward, he'll give a five-minute rebuttal." — Jay Leno

---

Can I Be Saved By Voting Repugnicant?

• Question From: Isabel Saggucci, Flowergirl, Faro, TX

SNIT'S RESPONSE: Absolutely! God has made his endorsement clear. (See "Authentic" letter from God in the beginning of this babble) as irrefutable evidence to this effect. But this still begs the question, what can you do to please God even more in the way of

support for Repugnicance. As the picture above illustrates, the path of getting saved requires that you are willing to walk across the narrow bridge above a fog of doubt and despair. This is the point we find ourselves in at this stage of the Obama Presidency. You must cast aside this doubt and walk across this bridge to a better nowhere that awaits us in the land of Repugnicance. Remember that all the great leaders of the world were once unknowns before they became known. I know how to create jobs. And Obama doesn't have a clue. To be saved, you need to start with clues. I have a sure fire political ideology (See My Secret Seven Point Plan) based on actual clues about how the economy works. Atheists without a birth certificate don't understand this. Doubters will not be saved unless they get with the program and support Repugnicance, and our famously fervent believe system in the supremacy of the free market economy.

How Soon Will the World End?

• Question From: Gail Baker, Dog Walker, Sante Fe, New Mexico.

SNIT'S RESPONSE: It depends! There are positive signs that may forestall the end of the world for at least a few more years, 10 years tops, unless I'm elected. Then things will get better, pronto.

But if we choose the other less preferred stock in Obama, this timetable could be speeded up. President Obooma clearly is not helping things. This fact was substantiated by Pastor Sedgewick Snodgrass in his sermon delivered to the Coon Creek Mormon Church, on the occasion of God's attendance in the front row pew much to the rapture of the other churchgoers. In a nutshell, what Pastor Snodgrass said was that we can't take the continuance of the future for granted.

He explained that eternity, in a technical sense is just beginning. But on a deeper analysis, we learn that God is not specific about eternities entry point and exit point in time. If it happens that we are about to exit from eternity prematurely, what is there to prevent

that from happening without **any** advance notice? See the picture to the left to realize just how close we are now to this possible exit point from eternity. The implications of this are profound. We must recognize that our decisions now will affect what happens henceforth. We have the power to control the future, because God's will is based upon our choice of the paths that lie before us. You can either choose to be pessimistic about the future or choose my more optimistic brand of Repugnicance. The choice is up to you.

Who is The True God of Repugnicance?

• Question From: Joe Patterson, Sheet Metal Worker, Detroit, MI

SNIT'S RESPONSE: Good question … Repugnicance is God, incarnated? Why else did God create Repugnicance as his only given political philosophy? God often hires ghosts, saints and disciples like me to do the heavy lifting on earth so that he can concentrate on improving heaven. So it is with Repugnicance and our ghosts. The Repugnicant ~~Bible~~ Babble makes pointed reference to some of the imponderables that we urge you to consider in considering who to trust. Either way blasphemy is nothing to be sneezed at.

In the Repugnicance Movement we believe that our saints have been anointed by God and history to lead us to the promised land of Repugnant Bliss. We believe that Repugnicance is God's will incarnate. There is a close bondage here. God is Repugnicance Repugnicance is God …. They are one and the same. Because of this we cannot lose the election? Just ask God. He knows!

Why are Democraps Such Snobs?

• Question From: Ben Sadka, Dirt Farmer, Aggra, CO

SNIT'S RESPONSE: I have known some Democraps who say, "Our candidates are more smarter than Repugnicants." They can't even get their punctuation right. Simply because Repugnicants have had a few "oops" moments during our debates, they jump all over our intelligence quotient. Obviously, Democraps are elite snobs.

 ... This is their way of trying to rationalize their sorry plight by portraying themselves as "intellectually superior." Unfortunately this perception has taken hold in some portions of the "liberal" media. Let me caution all Repugnicants against appearing "intellectual" in public. It's a futile gesture. It's also a risky maneuver, politically because it will expose you as members of the resistance. With the inspired political leadership of Ronald Reagan, George Bush, John McCain and now me, intellectualism will soon become a vestige of previous civilizations on earth. But until that glorious day, we must be careful how we appear in public. As we perfect our abilities of insincere manipulation in both our public and private personas, we are doing our part to insure that the overpowering forces of pretense and manipulation have their way. Now some of you of may find yourself regressing into intellectuality occasionally. Don't let it happen. I warn you. We don't want to be perceived as intelligent. It just goes over the heads of most voters.

What is the Best Way to Root Out Subversives from Within Our Society?

• Question From: Ruth Poop, Secretary, Madison WI

SNIT'S RESPONSE: The best way to root out subversives is to support Repugnicant's proposed legislation to expand the Patriot Act to include "Liberals as Terrorists." If you're like most Repugnicance Patriots, you have trouble sleeping in

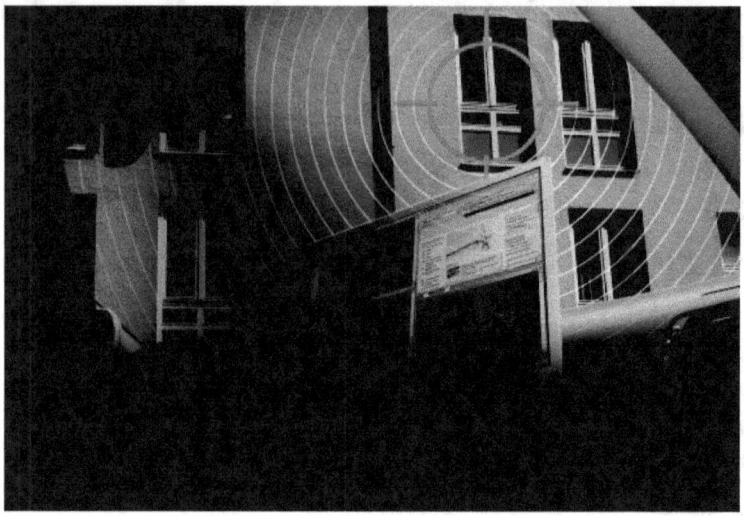

fear that desperate liberals and Democrapic subversives are now working towards a dismantling of the American values and our fabric of life. We all pray fervently for the fate of our nation and then leave voice and email messages with other Repugnicants seeking to create a viral effect of paranoia. Eventually these prayers and voice mail messages will be transmitted wirelessly to the Repugnicance Database, which will be included and funded by the Repugnicance Patriot Act. We will then transmit these paranoid messages to God, who will act through his omniscient powers to create a groundswell of political support for a much needed redefinition of civil liberty.

Was Barack Obama's Election an Abortion?

• Question From: Wally the Wave, 19, Surferdude, San Diego, CA

SNIT'S RESPONSE: AN EMPHATIC YES!!!! Barack Obooma's election to the Presidency was plain and simply an abortive departure from the norm. Never before in the history of human politics has a man with so many quirks been elected to the highest office in our land's country. Look how he sips beer.

This is not normal. George Bush, who admittedly was not necessarily the ideal personage for the job of President, at least knew how to guzzle. Don't be tricked by those grandiose speeches Obama made that entranced a nation and world with his mesmerization powers. This is the stuff of demagoguery not to mention socialism. But this begs the question of how he elected himself and Joe Biddle as his sidekick with the support of so many normally common sensical people voting. Was it because he was a celebrity? It defies the imagination to consider the root causes of this anomaly. A more plausible explanation of this aberrance would simply to dismiss Obama's election as being "Not George Bush!"

If this is the case than what does it say about this country? It is not good to say the least. We have to make America strong again. Barack Obama is a sissy who apologies for everything. His delectability is all about abortive departures. We have to put this country back on the path to greatness, and with Repugnicant campaign coffers jiggling we'll get them this time. It's a the dawning of a new day for America…. It's morning in America … it's either or both.

What, If Anything, Do You Read?

• Question From: Ruth Cannister, Bookeeper, Richmond, VA

SNIT'S RESPONSE: I really enjoy reading spreadsheets. I find them endless fascinating and revealing about which way a company is headed and where we can save money. With regard to other forms of literature, I urge caution. Reading is a hazardous exercise. One should never attempt to read without wearing a helmet If you have an accident, while reading it can result in intelligence and (in extreme circumstances) lead to ideas.

But let's back up a bit. This is the perfect example of a gotcha question, planted by the mainstream media to detract from me and my natural charisma. The snobs in the elite media constantly put down our

Repugnicance as religion-lite. This is because they read. Some of them even read books. (And I'm not talking about comic books). They read books that are much too long. The Repugnicant ~~Bible~~ Babble does not recommend reading anything other than t-shirts, bumperstickers and tweets. Anything longer than 140 character is extraneous and can cause the Repugnicant mind to buckle. That said we recommend wearing glasses to give the appearance of erudition. Take Saint Sarah for example. She doesn't need to wears glasses, but she does! When asked what he regularly reads, P. Rick Perry anticipated the trap and gave the perfect response: "all of them" so as not to be typecast as a rote conservative or even worse – a liberal.

Snit Romney's
"Secret Seven"
Point Agenda

MANY PEOPLE WONDER EXACTLY WHAT KIND OF SECRET PLAN MITT ROMNEY HAS IN STORE FOR US, BOTH IN HIS CAMPAIGN AND SHOULD HE BECOME PRESIDENT. HERE ARE ARE THE "SECRET SEVEN" POINTS OF SNIT'S AGENDA.

Point 1 - Growth Through Innovation

Snit's plan to stimulate the economy begins with innovation. He will introduce new technologies and market them through brand building campaigns much like the Romney brand is being marketed to American voters. As a "successful businessman" at the help of Bain Capital, Snit specialized in finding companies that were underperforming and turning them around by spinning off whole divisions and selling them. One such company, that hasn't received much attention was an Ohio based firm that produced an innovative device called the "Stupidity Siphon."

Bain brought in marketers who set up distribution channels through major retail outlets such as Wal-Mart, Best Buy, Sears and Macys. They tapped into the "nostalgia craze" by positioning it as a 21st century version of the home bomb shelter that was all the rage in the 1950's. One of the truly innovative items in the SS starter kit was a simple but elegant device that enabled ordinary citizens to harvest rainwater for emergency drinking supplies by employing inexpensive plastic tubing to create a "Premium Grade Stupidity Siphon." This ingenious technology collected rainwater in buckets (placed at the bottom of drain spouts), siphoning water upwards towards 50-gallon drums (available also in 100 gallon and 500 gallon sizes) and was placed on the roof, not unlike the box I transported Seamus in on trips. But these drums were designed to be used alternatively for hot tubs and bathing. Bain's PR team created animated commercials with Super Heros using the stupidity siphon as a metaphor for modern life, creating a closed loop of infinite societal stupidity. As President, Snit plans to replicate this "success story" in industries all across the economic spectrum.

Point 2 - Strengthen the Bonds of Finance

In Snit Romney's Secret Plan, creative finance is the key to a rejuvenated economy. As money managers go, so goes the economy. Making the right connections through bonds is essential for those who work in Club Wall Street. To strength and stabilize the financial sector, Snit's economic team will introduce new financial instruments including innovative "Derivative Financial Bonds." The precise mechanics of how DFBs will work is being kept under wraps, but we have learned that it involves creating leveraged time share between members of Club Wall Street, who will then be able to spend time in each others second, third, fourth, fifth and sixth homes.

The economic benefits of these Bonds of Finance have been questioned by experts, but vigorously defended by private equity executives as the most cost effective use of government stimulus dollars with the ultimate goal of stock portfolio appreciation.

Point 3 - Snit's Signal Plan For Dog Lovers

It's no secret that Snit Romney has suffered mega PR fallout as a result of the infamous Seamus Romney dog on-the-roof episode. In his campaign for President, Snit Romney's consultants have come up with a plan to turn a liability into an asset by reaching out to dog lovers with a fun loving a Repugnicant bonding signal.

The greeting is subtle, but unmistakable. Cup your hands up around your face like an excited canine and bark, "Wuff, Wuff" several times. Alternatively, dog lovers might choose to use the our Approval Response Rating Formula (AARF) and bark, "AARF, AARF" instead. The campaign brochure elaborates, "Whenever you see someone in a supermarket checkout line who you think may be Repugnicant, smile and offer Snit's Secret Greeting with a muted barking sound. If they respond with a "Snit Signal," you have created a lastingly Repugnicant bond." The somewhat controversial plan will be aggressively promoted through paid political advertisements, community focus groups, church networks and board meetings.

Point 4 - Retool by Promoting Monopoly

Snit Romney also has plan to reach out to those discouraged citizens who are out of work. Snit, with an instinctive empathy for those less fortunate, recognizes that these people often have a lot of time on their hands. He understands that they may be angry and bitter that the engine of the economy has sputtered in their lives. He recognizes that it doesn't have to be like this. All it takes for these people to become productive members of society is a little mental retooling. To prepare citizens for the transitions that await them, the Snit Romney Team has developed a re-tooling module based upon a new improved version bored game of "Monopoly."

In this digitally revised and reversed version of the venerable bored game, participants start with a full portfolio of bank stocks, US Government securities and real estate assets. As the economy tanks under Obama's inept leadership, the banks and auto companies get government bailouts. Their stocks soar. When the "inflate" card is chosen, federal deficits become so large that the government must default. The stock market then crashes, the federal government declares bankruptcy and all stocks, bonds and real estate assets become worthless. Club Wall Street then buys the assets for pennies on the dollar and government stimulus funds revive the economy creating huge gains for investors. It's a fun filled way of coming to grips with the potential tragedy inherent in Obama economic program. Snit's Bain colleagues, who were tipped in advance to divest their portfolio and stash their money is Swiss bank accounts will become fabulously wealthy while the rest of the players become destitute and go to jail.

Point 5 - Flush Leftish Propaganda

In order for free the market to function effectively, Team Snit has recognized the need to stem the alarming rise of radical liberalism. Towards this end Snit has developed a digital self-composting toilet designed to take eco-liberal bullshit and flush it down the toilet of pubic consciousness so that it can't be used in any future campaigns.

As head of Bain Capital, Snit became adept at dealing with environmental extremists who were always crying wolf about what they call the "overwhelming stress" human activities have placed upon our ecological system. Snit's

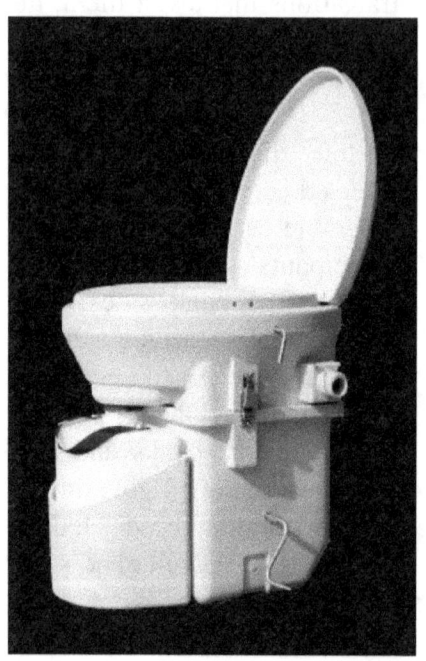

Secret Plan takes this one step further with a device to flush eco-waste of Democrapic ideas. Team Snit believes that Repugnicant funded public relations efforts can actually flush all Democrapic rhetoric down the toilet of all mainstream media outlets. The ultimate eco-Democrap, Al Bore is the chief target of these digitally self composting toilets.

Needless to say, Al Bore's eco-cronies have been pushing back and some of the Democrap has been coming back up through the Internet ether. Team Snit however has a secret plan for a "National Flush" in which all the intellectual Democrapic BS, including rhetoric about the need for reduced defense spending, getting rid of tax cuts for the rich and reduced anti-terrorism campaigns are flushed vigorously and often by Fox News and other Repugnicant media outlets.

Point 6 - Take U. S. Inc. Public

Snit Romney believes that owning stock in corporate America is the key to making America strong again. His economic advisors know that Obama's economic brain mistrust, with their "anti-business" agenda, has taken the exact opposite course leading to the unraveling of the global economy. Team Snit's secret plan is to prepare for complete transfer of all remaining assets on Main Street to Wall Street with the formation of U.S. Inc.. The IPO will be registered on Day One of the Romney presidency, and will publicly announced at the inauguration ceremoney (sic). The U. S. Inc. capital structure is patterned after the Facebook cash out model. Investors are salivating over the first day pop, with mega upside in this new phase of American economic history. Stock in many major corporate entities like Bank of America, Goldman Sachs, GE and Citicorp will be exchangeable with shares in this great country of ours.

This is only the first phase of a larger plan. Snit's team is thinking anew and afar in constructing more healthy and enduring financial instruments and economic relationships. Soon the entire U. S. economy will simply be a subsidiary of U.S Inc. and all citizens of sufficient means can become stockholders with all the privileges of ownership in U. S. Inc.. Insiders will be able to get in on the ground floor of this exciting venture by purchasing equity in Snit. Inc. with campaign contributions which can later be converted into "preferred" shares of U. S. Inc. through secondary markets. Buy now and watch the value of your shares pop at the opening bell, on Inauguration day.

Point 7 - Promote Darwinian Finance

Snit Romney, like all true Repugnicants is a Darwinian who believes in the survival of the fittest. The world of Private Equity, where Snit survived is in actuality a modern day version of the primitive era of civilization when cavemen and apes roamed the earth and asserted their superiority on the basis of brute force alone. Instead of using sticks and clubs, they use the instruments of high finance.

Point 7 in Snit Romney secret plan calls for formal recognition of this new era in survivalism. Towards this end, Team Snit will replace the Swearing in Ceremony with an initiation rite into Romney postmodern era. This era will create a dawning of new finance where are Private Equity creatures, will live happily ever after in their gated caves, mansions and moated castles. The initiation rites of this new Darwinian era can be likened to the snoring phase that usually concludes Harvard Club events. Like other initiation rites throughout this passage in time, theses rites will reassert feudalist control structures where debt becomes the instrument for enslavement of the masses. This truly is the dawning of a new era. Remember a vote for Snit is a vote for Darwin. If Snit Romney is elected, it will be crowning achievement of the annual Darwin awards for stupidity.

About the Author - John F. Ince

John F. Ince has re-invented himself multiple times in his career and sooner or later he hopes to get it right. At various times he has been a reporter, banker, author, satirist, social entrepreneur, journalist, blogger, podcaster, video producer, photographer, documentary filmmaker and wizard. In more recent life, he is founder / CEO of The Credit  Commons and Moneeey, Inc.. He previously worked as a reporter for *Fortune Magazine*, as a contributing editor with *Upside Magazine* and as a casewriter at Harvard Business School and Harvard's John F. Kennedy School of Government. Before that he worked for Sea Pines Company and on Wall Street with Chase Manhattan Bank. He served as an aide to former Senator Paul Tsongas organizing a U.S. Senate caucus for solar energy. He has founded two non profits, One World Inc. and The Earth Aid Foundation. He is the author of The Earth Pledge and organized the Earth Pledge Campaign in conjunction with the 25th anniversary celebration of Earth Day. Belief it or not, he is an honors graduate of Harvard College where he was First Marshal (President) of his graduating class. He also, amazingly, received his MBA from Harvard Business School in Finance. Please check out the companion books this series ...

Mitt Romney

The King of Bain

and the Man Who Wants To Be the
The President

By John F. Ince

THE
WIZ OF IZ

A STORY ABOUT THE POWER OF INSPIRED LEADERSHIP, THE BIRTH OF A MOVEMENT AND THE TRIUMPH OF

HOPE

JOHN F. INCE

Repugnicants

The Wacky World of Republican Politics

Featuring:

Snoot Gingrich, Snit Romney, Run Paul,
P.Rick Perry, Michele Babblethump,
Herman Pizza and Donald Dump

BY
JOHN F. INCE

Repugnicance

The 2012 Version of the Republican Bible Babble

Edited and Curated by

George Won't
Columnist for the *Washington Pissed*

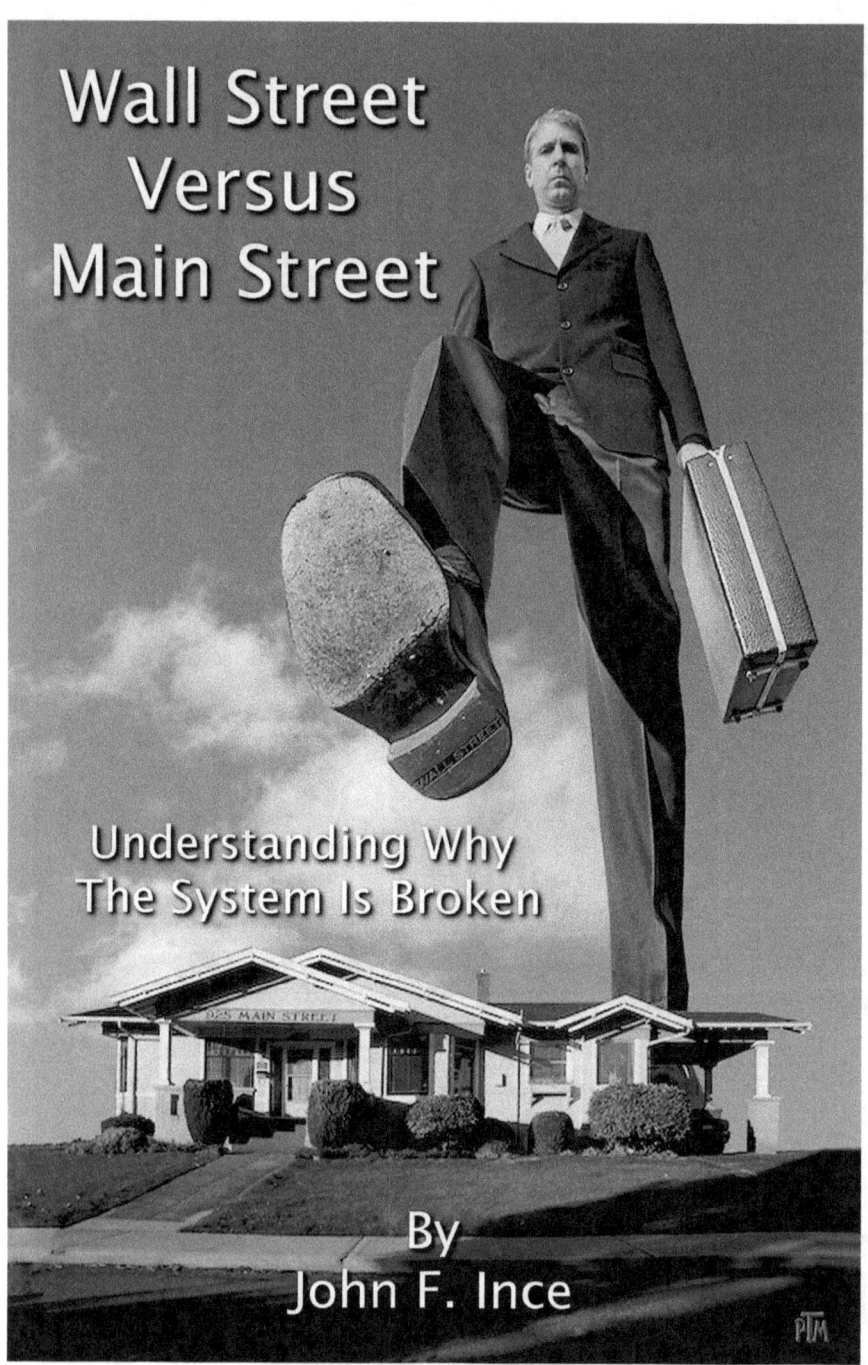

Wall Street Versus Main Street

Understanding Why The System Is Broken

By
John F. Ince

Main Street
Versus
Wall Street

Transforming Raw Anger
Into Purposeful Action

John F. Ince

Sarah Palin

Going ~~Rogue~~
Rude

The Official Handbook of the
Sarah Palin Admiration Society

Sarah Palin

Going ~~Rogue~~
Bogus

The Official Handbook of the
Sarah Palin Admiration and Salvation Society

Snit Romney ... Going Going Viral

Use these links as touchstones to the rapture.

Snit Romney on Twitter:
@SnitRomney or #Snit

Snit Romney's Facebook Page:
www.SnitRomney.net

Snit Romney's Blog: www.SnitRomney.org

Snit Romney on Amazon: www.SnitRomney.com

REpugnicance: www.repugnicance.com

www.ingramcontent.com/pod-product-compliance
Lightning Source LLC
Chambersburg PA
CBHW072339290526
45794CB00002B/946